AF448472

Written by Adam Starks, Ph.D.

Illustrated by Natasha Payne-Brunson

Cover Art by Natasha Payne-Brunson

Published by Adam Starks, Ph.D.

ISBN: 979-8-21823-922-0 (paperback)

ISBN: 979-8-21823-923-7 (digital)

Printed in the United States of America

This book is dedicated to my sister, Eve.

I've always admired your free spirit and tenacity.

Thank you for being such a loving sister and

being part of my good childhood memories.

Love Makes The World Go 'Round

Written by Adam Starks, Ph.D.
Illustrated by Natasha Payne-Brunson

Every child waiting on their place to call home has the potential to do spectacular things! If we can instill hope and tap into their resilience, their dreams are possible!

Love knew I loved animals and placed a puppy and toy veterinary kit in front of me when I was only 9 years old.

Today, I am a successful vet with dreams of starting a clinic one day!

Love gave me a toy plane when I was just 8 years old.

She told me that I would rule the clouds one day.

Today, my plane is so much bigger. Thanks to Love, I am a pilot for a major airliner flying people all over the world!

Love always told me that my past didn't define me. He always reminded me that I had a helping heart, and the world was my oyster.

Today, I am a counselor for recovering addicts so I can do my part to make sure others don't have to grow up like I did. With my help, they have access to the treatment they need to heal their minds and bodies.

Love instilled an interest in coding by letting me tinker with his laptop programs.

He noticed my gift for creating new code and discovering new ways to protect it.

CY
SEC

Thanks to his encouragement, I am a sought-after Cyber Security Engineer and Consultant who teaches other agencies to protect their data all over the globe!

Love always let me play with her stethoscope, and my foster siblings usually let me check their heartbeats!

She said I had healing hands and always accepted my diagnosis.

That pretend play gave me the confidence to be head nurse at a children's hospital. I also accompany doctors on medical mission trips spreading my healing hands far and wide.

Love always told me that I would be a remarkable man one day as long as I ignored the naysayers.

He noticed my interest in numbers and need to nurture others.

Thanks to him, I'm the CEO of a non-profit that ensures no teen slips through the cracks.

As they approach emancipation, they will have all the resources they need to succeed under my watch.

Ever since my first birthday, I was fascinated by fire trucks.

Love took time to play in my imagination world
and even build a fire station with blocks!

CITY OF SPAR
13
FIRE DEPARTME

Now I'm a Fire Chief and established a safe haven program for unwanted babies. Today, I'm as brave as I was alone in the dumpster, but I always have family standing right beside me.

Thanks to them, we achieved what others thought was impossible. Through our trauma-informed community, we had the resources we needed to attend a trade school or college.

This will always be YOUR home! I promise you the safety and security that comes with being loved. You will never be neglected as you figure out life and make it on your own. No matter what happens, we will always be here for you and committed to your success!

Dream brightly and remember that no miracle should ever hide their gifts. Make the world a better place by sharing your love with others through your talented hands and minds.

About the Author

Dr. Adam Starks is a shining example of resilience in the face of adversity. Having grown up in the foster care system, he knows first-hand the challenges that young people in similar situations face trying to access social services and mental wellness resources. After aging out of the system, Dr. Starks earned a bachelor's degree from Eastern Mennonite University, an **MBA** from Strayer University, and a **Ph.D.** in Organizational Leadership from Capella University. Driven by his experiences, he is now the Founder and **CEO** of MNDYRR (mender), a platform that helps at-promise youth achieve their full potential.

As an inspirational keynote speaker on foster care, child mental health and trauma-informed care. Dr. Starks advocates for vulnerable communities and actively serves on the local school board and as President of the West Virginia CASA Association board. He resides in Philippi, West Virginia with his wife and three children.

About the Illustrator

Natasha Payne-Brunson is a graphic designer and librarian who enjoys expressing her creativity through illustration. She holds a Bachelor of Fine Arts degree in painting and printmaking from Virginia Commonwealth University and a Master of Science in Library Science from Clarion University. Natasha is known for her artistic flair and referred to as the "artsylibrarian". Alongside her husband and two boys, she resides in Richmond, Virginia, and you can contact her at npbrunsondesigns@gmail.com.